THE LIVING WATERS

OF BUDDHISM

BRIAN TAYLOR

道

UNIVERSAL OCTOPUS

Also available:

What is Buddhism?
Buddhism and Drugs
The Five Buddhist Precepts
Basic Buddhist Meditation
Basic Buddhism for a World in Trouble
Dependent Origination
The Ten Fetters (Saŋyojana)
Buddhist Pali Chants (with English translations)
The Five Nivāraṇas
(Buddha's Teaching of the Five Hindrances)

Published by Universal Octopus 2017
www.universaloctopus.com

ISBN 978-1-9999063-0-6

"The purpose of the Holy Life does not consist in acquiring alms, honour, or fame, nor in gaining morality, concentration, or knowledge and vision. The object of the Holy Life, its essence, its goal is unshakeable liberation of mind."

THE LIVING WATERS OF BUDDHISM

Turn on the tap. Out comes water. Mix it with tea leaves and call it Tea. Mix it with coffee grains and call it Coffee. Mix it with fermented hops and call it Beer. Mix it with coloured pigments and call it Paint.

Mix it with arsenic and call it Poison.

Water is cool, refreshing and necessary to sustain life. But what is mixed with it can change its nature, making it not cool, not refreshing, even inimical to life. It can be made to stimulate, inflame or even kill.

Buddhism is the cool water of the universe. It is refreshing. It sustains the holy life. It revives the parched heart of man.

But as it flows from its fountainhead in Bodhi Gaya, it becomes mixed with other things. It becomes Mahayana, Theravada, Yogacara, Soto, Zen. It is mixed with national and racial characteristics. There is Indian Buddhism, Thai Buddhism, Ceylonese Buddhism, Japanese Buddhism, Chinese Buddhism, Tibetan Buddhism. Even American and English Buddhism.

It also gets mixed with cultural and aesthetic additives. You find Buddhist painting, Buddhist literature, Buddhist sculpture, Buddhist iconography, Buddhist drama, Buddhist poetry. It has even been mixed with martial arts. Martial arts kill.

Many of these national and cultural flowerings of Buddhism are of interest in their own right. They tell us a great deal about the peoples and societies that have produced them. But it is sometimes difficult to discern the living water of Buddhism itself. Just as it is difficult to distinguish the distinctive qualities of water in, say, a glass of whisky which is fiery, burning, intoxicating and parches the palate.

With water you refer back to the basic structure of water. Two parts Hydrogen. One part Oxygen. Everything else, whatever its merits, is not water.

With Buddhism it is the same. What are the basic teachings of Buddha himself? Not Guru This or Acharn That.

Fortunately, the Buddha's teachings have been very well preserved in the language that he spoke himself.

The Pali Language has been thoroughly investigated and explained by many fine scholars in different cultures over a long period. Although there will always be different opinions as to how best to translate some of the Buddha's concepts into different modern languages, there is general agreement as to what these concepts mean.

In addition, although the Buddha touched on different subjects and used a variety of images to illustrate what he was saying, the main themes are repeated again and again in sutta[1] after sutta.

---

[1] Sutta: *A discourse given by the Buddha or one of his senior disciples.*

Even the same logical sequences, which link these themes in an organised whole, are continually restated in sutta after sutta.

To what effect?

The Buddha begins with the unsatisfactoriness of Life as living beings actually experience it.

He then demonstrates what is the cause of this unsatisfactoriness.

Then he indicates that there _is_ a state of Total Freedom and Happiness, which is permanent and unchanging.

Finally, and most important of all for those of us who wish to _do_ something about our predicament, he outlines a simple step-by-step method by which the state of perfection can be reached by any sincere and normal human being.

The living water of Buddhism is this method, which quenches the thirst of a suffering world.

The other things which have accrued to Buddhism - artistic, cultural, ceremonial, philosophical, nationalist additions - may well have merit in themselves but they are not Buddhism and they need to be clearly distinguished from Buddhism.

To the anthropologist this may not seem important. He takes things as he finds them and he tracks their development.

But for the practitioner who wishes to do what the Buddha says should be done for one's own welfare, it is essential to be clear about the basic Buddhism that the Buddha actually taught.

It was to liberate beings, not to educate them in other ways, that the Buddha arose from his Samādhi[2].

As is stated in the Majjhima–Nikāya (The Middle Length Sayings), Sutta 29:

> **"The purpose of the Holy Life does not consist in acquiring alms, honour, or fame, nor in gaining morality, concentration, or knowledge and vision. The object of the Holy Life, its essence, its goal is unshakeable liberation of mind."**

It is necessary from the outset to be clear in one's own mind that one wants this "liberation of mind". A man drinks whisky not to quench his thirst but to enflame his senses. He drinks not for the water itself but for the alcohol for which the water is just a carrying agent.

Similarly a man can study Buddhist art because he is interested in art. He can study the Pali language because he is interested in languages or poetry or history. If he does this he will not become liberated, nor will he want to be. Just as the drinker of whisky will not have his thirst quenched, nor will he want this.

But a man who does want to be liberated will seek out the pure essence of Buddhism just as a thirsty man will seek pure water. And the pure essence of Buddhism presents a method for achieving, once and for all, this "unshakeable liberation of mind".

---

[2] Samādhi: *State of Perfect Peace and Calm.*

It is compared to cool, living water because the opposite of liberation is bondage. Bondage, as far as the human mind is concerned, has the characteristics of heat and passion.

Heat and passion accompany grasping after experience and sensation.

The world, said the Buddha, is on fire; burning. Burning with craving, anger, hatred, envy, frustration, excitement, fear, remorse, disappointment.

We can see this for ourselves. To be free from this, we need to liberate ourselves.

Liberate ourselves from what? From craving.

Why craving? Because it is craving which causes suffering in all its many forms by leading a man to grasp after the objects of his desires.

And the objects of his craving invariably betray him.

What are the objects of this craving? They are all the various phenomena of life itself. Things that are seen or heard or smelt or tasted or touched with this human body. And the human body itself, which is known by seeing, hearing, smelling, tasting and feeling. The whole physical universe is our body and the extensions of our body.

Without our bodies we would have no access to the physical universe and it would not exist for us.

Mental Objects, too, are objects of this craving. Thoughts, feelings, memories and imagination make up the mental universe and we use our minds to contact them. Without our minds we would have no access to this mental universe and it would not exist for us.

We have this body and this mind. They are constantly inter-reacting by way of cause and effect. Together they are the objects of this craving. We grasp after all the paraphernalia that make up mind and body, continually, incessantly, from moment to moment. And because we do this we put ourselves at the mercy of these things.

And we suffer.

We do not find lasting satisfaction in these things. We see things and they are unpleasant, so we experience dissatisfaction. We see pleasant things and they do not last, so we experience dissatisfaction. We see neutral things and we find them of no interest to us, so we experience dissatisfaction.

And this same pattern of dissatisfaction is experienced through the ear, the nose, the mouth and the sense of touch. And the mind. Moment to moment. Day and night. Month after month. Year after year. Lifetime after lifetime. There is no end to the flow of phenomena.

And there is no end to our consequential suffering if we continue to grasp after them.

The actual objects of our senses are not within our ultimate control. Nor are the senses themselves. We cannot make our eyes and ears last forever. We cannot ensure that pleasant experiences will occur when we want them to and last for as long as we want. We cannot ensure that we will remain free of unpleasant experiences.

We cannot say, "I choose not to be sick. Not to grow old. Not to die." So long as we are in contact with phenomena, we cannot be free of their characteristics.

We remain in contact with them because there is a grasping after them. Freedom comes when this grasping is replaced by a letting go. A letting go of the objects of sense and the objects of mind.

Control of these things is not within our power. "Unshakeable liberation" from them is.

We cannot prevent fire from burning our hands by telling it to be cool. Because the nature of fire is not to be cool. *But we can prevent our hands from reaching out and grasping after the fire.*

"The purpose of the Holy Life does not consist in acquiring alms, honour, or fame, nor in gaining morality, concentration, or knowledge and vision. The object of the Holy Life, its essence, its goal is unshakeable liberation of mind."

Pure water is hydrogen and oxygen. Nothing more. Pure Buddhism is the path to Liberation. Nothing more. A man who sees this clearly rouses himself and makes straight for his Eternal Home, Nibbāna.

Buddhism is straightforward and direct. It teaches cause and effect. Do this and that will result. Avoid this and that will cease.

What is of the utmost importance is to grasp the fact that, if the Buddha's instructions are scrupulously and honestly followed, the attainment of Nibbāna is assured for any human being who is reading this passage here and now.

If one deviates from the clear instructions, the goal is no longer assured. If one doesn't follow the map, one may end up somewhere else.

If one is half-hearted, if one changes the rules to fit in with Thai customs, English customs, American customs, Tibetan customs, Japanese customs, Chinese customs, the goal is no longer assured.

If one attempts to blend Buddhism with modern science, with contemporary ideas, with politics, with sociology, the goal is no longer assured.

Pure Buddhism is direct and clear. Do this, achieve that.

Do what?

The Buddha has told us how to walk, how to stand, how to sit and how to lie down. We are told to do all these mindfully and with clear comprehension. He has told us how to eat, how to attend to the needs of the body. Mindfully.

He teaches us to be aware of what we are doing now, how we are doing it, why we are doing it and what the results of doing it will be.

He has told us how to *speak:* honestly, straightforwardly and without harsh language, slander, gossip or vain talk.

He has told us how to *behave* in our dealings with the world and with others. We should not kill, or steal, or betray our wives and husbands, or lie and deceive. We should avoid alcohol and drugs because they cause carelessness and carelessness leads to suffering for ourselves and others.

He has told us how to *earn a living*. We should support ourselves in ways which are honest and do not cause suffering. We should not trade in living beings, or weapons. We should not be butchers. We should not sell alcohol or intoxicating drugs or poisons.

He has told us how to *think*. We should empty our minds of negative and unprofitable thoughts. We should develop positive states of mind; compassion, friendliness, diligence, detachment, patience, generosity, perseverance.

We should develop understanding and wisdom.

He has shown that the highest understanding is reached by seeing that life, as it is experienced by all beings, has three fundamental characteristics. It is not satisfactory, it is impermanent and it has nothing in it which is ourselves or belongs to ourselves.

Moreover, and most usefully, he has explained that life is not chaotic or random in the way it works but proceeds by cause and effect, which he calls Karma.

Karma means "doing", "action". Its opposite is not doing, no action.

Everything which is done, proceeds by cause and effect. I drop the cup, it breaks. I press the switch, the light comes on.

Nothing is random. If I sow carrot seeds, I get carrots. I don't get parsnips. If I press the wall next to the switch, the light doesn't come on.

All around us in the world and inside us in our minds what we see are the effects of innumerable causes. The houses we live in, the people we associate with, environmental problems, the clothes we wear, the thoughts and memories we have, our ideas and opinions, our physical fitness.

We can recognise a lot of this. Buddhism takes it further and says, *all* phenomena are the results of causes.

But the effects of causes are also the causes of future effects.

I make a sculpture. From this I make a mould. The mould is used to make more sculptures. The carrots grow; their seed will produce more carrots. My thoughts are the cause of more thoughts, or words, or actions. Cause and effect are two aspects of the same thing seen at different points in time. This is Karma.

This is most important in the realm of ethics. Just as a good seed produces a good plant, so a good deed means a good result.

> *The Law is mirror-like in its precision*
> *and its simplicity needs no revision;*
> *that Good breeds Good*
> *and Evil has its price;*
> *that Virtue is its own reward.*
> *And so is Vice.*

Those who cannot see the connection between cause and effect are often too hasty.

Like the small boy who, hearing that an acorn would grow into an oak tree, planted his acorn and came back a week later looking for his oak tree. "It doesn't work," he said.

It is easier to chop down
an acorn
than an oak.

(The branch you bang
your head on
is an acorn
that you missed.)

Here and now we are surrounded by a world of effects. Here and now everything we think and say and do acts as a cause and will produce corresponding effects.

We are free to choose.

We have inherited the past. We can create a future we would like to inherit. Starting with our own thoughts and intentions. Fundamental to this process is; do good, get good; do bad, get bad.

Right understanding also means seeing that things which are unsatisfactory, impermanent and have nothing in them that is ourselves or which belongs to us, can never bring us happiness.

If we continue to grasp after things which we cannot control and which are bound to let us down, we cannot realise and experience Nibbāna, the eternal, peaceful state which is the end of all suffering.

Buddha has provided us with a straightforward method by which we can train our minds to realise Nibbāna ourselves – Vipassanā. Insight Meditation[3].

---

[3] *See* Basic Buddhist Meditation *ISBN 978-0-9956346-9-5*
Available through www.universaloctopus.com

What we need to do is put our understanding into practice. For ourselves. Without delay. For the mind that is reading this at this moment does not know how much longer life will last.

This is the pure water of Buddhism; the message of Liberation and the Path leading to it.

Anything else, the statues, the incense, the pictures, the costumes, the ceremonies, the fortune-telling, the adaptations to suit different cultural and national backgrounds, the involvement in politics or social welfare, or linguistic studies - all these are of great interest to the student of life, but they are not pure Buddhism.

Pure Buddhism is the Living Water of the Universe. Who will drink it?

THE QUIET MIND

The sun
shines
in a bucket of water

but doesn't
get
wet.

www.ingramcontent.com/pod-product-compliance
Lightning Source LLC
Chambersburg PA
CBHW020451030426
42337CB00014B/1496